Masked

Masked

JOHNNIE MAE BOUTWELL

RESOURCE *Publications* • Eugene, Oregon

MASKED

Resource Publications
An Imprint of Wipf and Stock Publishers
199 W. 8th Ave., Suite 3
Eugene, OR 97401

www.wipfandstock.com

PAPERBACK ISBN: 979-8-3852-2612-2
HARDCOVER ISBN: 979-8-3852-2613-9
EBOOK ISBN: 979-8-3852-2614-6

08/06/24

The characters and events portrayed in this book are fictitious. Any similarity to real persons, living or dead, is coincidental and not intended by the author.

To Daniel, and all the friends I don't know how to keep. . .

Contents

EQUAL TO MY DARKEST NIGHT

What a peculiar and masochistic soul I am.

That I would rifle through the depths of my own agony,

and unearth the records of my own heartbreak.

I, stubborn creature that I am,

cannot let alone the wounds that riddle my tattered and bedraggled soul.

Forever I poke and prod at my own inadequacies,

like a child pulling at the ear that pains it.

Longing and searching and pressing harder

until I am numb to that which once crippled me,

and can gaze upon my life's horrors with the cool practiced glare of a clinician.

Cutting out that which is like cancer

and throwing it away from myself.

Taking this here and putting it there.

Dragging from the depths the harsh truths of my own depravity,

and thrusting them into the light of my conscious and reason to be judged.

As if to say, "Look! Here! This is the beast that you are! This is all that is the best of you."

In this way I judge myself,

weigh my own worth,

and find myself lacking in all the things that I admire.

My deepest fear that I will one day become all the things which I hate is realized,

belatedly with the sure knowledge that what I have hated I have hated because it has always been what I am.

That the only becoming I have done has been the slow uncovering
   and systematic destruction of the worst parts of myself,
stretching over a lifetime.
Until I am left empty,
A hollow husk,
Pouring beauty and art and dreams into myself.
Desperate that something, anything, some substance should stick,
should ignite in me some passion equal to my darkest night.

AT THE EDGE OF OBLIVION

So strange the human creature,

so disconnected from one another.

Are we merely facets of a single reality?

Or is my universe so far removed from others that I am as strange
and alien to them as they are to me?

Is it I who is disconnected, or was there never a connection to be
had?

We stand, unaware, at the edge of oblivion.

Lost in our ignorance.

A swirling multitude of separate consciousnesses unable to touch.

We rage and fight wars over ideas,

and our own chemically induced biological responses as though it
had some deeper meaning.

So terrified are we, of being insignificant, that we never stop to
consider that our ideas are all wrong.

We are the insignificant.

An unnoticed speck on someone else's horizon.

We stand in awe of a seemingly cold and empty void stretching
endlessly before us,

and imagining arrogantly, that it is ours.

I WONDER

Her image haunts me.
A tormented dream that I cannot render.
Beauty trapped at my fingertips.
I often wonder who she is?
I sit and give her names,
and wile away the hours in fanciful imaginings of her.
As I smudge lines on thick paper,
and obscure her face in graphite shadow.
I wonder. . .

HEAVY ARMOR

She's losing control.
She's getting so far behind.
She can't keep up,
Not with five-second-long minutes,
And not with perfect human molds.
They're dragging her down,
though she'll never let it show.
She keeps her head propped high,
with a patchwork lattice,
made of delicate dreams.
She'll take the punishment,
because she's learned the hard way,
Heavy armor just makes the pain that much harder to bear.

SWEET AGONY

Oh, such sweet agony
Such beautiful pain
To have for only one moment that which we cannot keep
To know it, and keep it still

HOPE

She's coming in and out of a haze.

Face dropping,

she's tired,

shoulders slumped.

Body aching,

she paints on her smile.

Trying to keep up with what's expected of her.

She's working her way up inch by inch,

and making her way forward.

Desperately trying to get back the hope she left behind when she
first started.

HEROS AND VULTURES

We have built corruption around our concept of the hero,
casting upon each savior the light of our suspicion.
We take sheep for wolves while the vultures wait. . .

FEAR

Most of what we fear is conjured within our own minds.
How astounding it is that we can know this and still be held captive
by it.

POISON IN THE WATER

Sometimes, we must exile the ones we love.
Sometimes, there is poison in the water.

SETTING FIRES

We run it seems on endless dreams.

Consumed by unsustainable desires.

Ignorant to our souls' screams,

That all we're doing is setting fires.

I sit in wonderment at my own ability to pretend,

That each false beginning won't have the same end.

I run forever at the same walls.

Caught forever in the same falls.

Too impatient to just wait.

Too stubborn to give in to hate.

I play a game with no rules,

And know at heart that I am with fools.

OVERCOMING

When most people hear the stories,

they talk about how strong and powerful I must have been.

But the truth is that nothing about my perceived strength is worthy of praise.

I took a jagged blade to the worst parts of myself

and hacked them away like a cancerous disease.

Desperate to be rid of what I thought made me weak.

I compromised the integrity of my foundation so thoroughly that the best of me was left to sink down into the gaping holes I had created.

But for those who were there, the truth, when they hear it, is too much for them to bear,

so that they deny the existence of what was once my reality.

I am dramatic.

I am exaggerating.

I am exacerbating my own condition.

They refuse to acknowledge to themselves that while they preach,

someone asked them for help and was ignored.

That my own suicide was a daily thought,

that I could not bring myself to voice for fear of their continued accusation.

So that they could tell themselves that they were loving, if only I had said something.

In the end, what more is there to say?

STARDUST

Let us run through boundless stars,
and share in galaxies together.
Leave behind Earth's mortal scars,
and dance upon stardust forever.

TRAGEDY

"There is glory in our tragedy."
Words fell from ruby lips,
below eyes that blazed with fire.
Though what burned there was not desire. . .

MY HEART COMES WITH ME

I mask my face,
shroud my heart in stone.
Give me a moment,
I'll remember what it means to be alone.
Steel my spine,
shoulders strong.
Forced to believe,
I can withstand this wrong.
With feet made steady,
I make my way.
I'll live forever,
as I die every day.
My heart comes with me,
heavy in my chest.
Its never been home,
Its never known rest.

A BAD DAY

When the pain is so much it hurts to breathe,
And I can't depend on the people I need.
The forces of gravity conspire against me.
The laws of physics take a back seat to my misery.
My bones acquire the density of lead,
My blood, a thick sludge that refuses to be bled.
The world is full of light, wonder, and a promise I can't reach.
Blocked by an impenetrable force, I can't breach.
I want so desperately to remove this shroud of black depression,
But it clings to me; I am its obsession,
and I do not know why.

WHEN I DAYDREAM

I am a terrible, horrible, incorrigible romantic.

Gazing off into the distance as I await the verdict of the universe.

Unsettled and agonized that I do not yet know the answers.

What is so wrong with me then,

that I am still so unloved?

Is my mother correct?

Will I be alone forever?

How am I to bear that?

Every moment of every day that I am without the love of family is agony beyond agony,

and I despise this meaningless existence with every fiber of my being.

However, I cannot go back;

I cannot return to the oppressive. . .

I am lost, so lost for so long.

My heart aches, and I find myself whispering into my own soul words of my own discontent.

I have exiled myself here desperate to save my soul.

Unwilling to return, forever alone by virtue of the fact;

It was monsters that taught me how to love, and so my love is wrong.

Bear in mind the very essence of reality.

That each of us creates our own by varying perception,

and where one may see terror,

another may see beauty.

Where there is nothing, therein may also lie the meaning of life.

We beseech our fellow man to see what we see;

Call out to one another to believe what we believe.

Create factions and draw lines.

Mass produce excepted modes of behavior,

and so, establish the ever-elusive, yet all-powerful force we name Society.

We advocate individualism with exception,

that the individual may only be right so long as they fit into the cohesive whole.

So then must we conform?

Must I conform?

For the simple inescapable fact that I was born to a particular faction of a particular mode of thought?

Does it matter so little that we may not fit?

Must we slave away our lives in misery for little recognition of our virtues?

Simply accept that we are here failures, and then live our lives as such?

Is it to truly be required of us to turn our backs on the very nature of our beings for the illusion of community and therein success?

History is rife with figures who break from convention, held high and exalted for their rebellion.

Yet we condemn and oppress all those who come after and try?

Will acceptance come only after the deed is done, the life lived?

At every point in history, it is shown that each version of Society
believes that it is unequivocally right,

As it is shown, imperial fall after imperial fall,

that there is an inherent flaw.

This is seen clearly and taught to us all with forebodings of caution,

and we take it into our minds that,

"Yes, yes, this is true."

Still, it never reaches our hearts,

so that mistakes are continuously repeated.

History goes on, never changing.

Each generation tisking in shame at a past they will prove unable
to learn from.

Thus, factions are born, and lines are drawn as rebel souls languish
on and on and on.

CALL IT UNENDING LOVE

Bring me agony, bring me sorrows.

Bring me all of nevers tomorrows.

Poor deeply into me all that we shall never be.

Fill me up with dreams and illusion,

before you turn your back and pretend it wasn't a choreographed
  intrusion.

I am endless hope.

A deep well with no rope.

Give me fear, and pity, and terror.

I'll take it all into myself,

and be the burden bearer.

In your eyes I see the truth of my disgrace.

That my heart, my soul, were so easy for you to misplace.

Yet still, deceive me in wonder my precious dove.

Give me lies and call it unending love.

WANDERLUST

I am filled with wanderlust.

I am flowing
like the Milky Way
through a clear, cool night's sky,
crisp and close.

I feel if I lost my balance I could fall into it.

Plush is the sensation
as I haphazardly careen through the stars
all the way to where heaven meets the earth
and the Milky Way spills into the soft sea.

Inside I'm the kind of warm reserved for winter nights, electric
blankets, crackling fires and contented souls.

But I think I might lose my fingers and my toes.

The desperate piercing ice coats my lungs,
sharply stabbing with every shallow breath.

And I know;

I know this is death.

ZEPHYRS SWEET WORDS

It was through the wood that the wind came to me,
whispering sweet words and soft nothings,
in that breeze the valley flowers danced,
and doing so,
they spoke as if they knew me.
"You are enough to move me."

Carried over oceans with this gentle breeze,
the voice of island mountains, were calling out to me,
"You are enough to move me."

Through those same woods you chanced to walk,
and along a flowing wind sweet whispers grace your ears,
and carries you for miles.
And all the valley flowers,
dancing in the wind,
they speak as if they know you too.
"You are enough to move me."

And carried over oceans,
on this gentle breeze,
the voice of island mountains,
sing words much like these.
"You are enough to move me."

And with all the wood of the earth,
and every valley flower,
beneath every island mountain,
moving and dancing and whispering to you,
How can you not believe your dreams worth doing?

A THOUGHT #1

Sometimes I have to tell me to leave myself alone. . .

A THOUGHT #2

How precarious our emotions are;
Caught in the pendulum of influence.
Dependent upon and vulnerable to
the idiosyncrasies of others.

A THOUGHT #3

I get angry when I am really sad,
and make enemies of the people who hurt me.
Even when I know they are the only people in the world who will
ever love me. . .

A THOUGHT #4

I almost prefer to die of loneliness.
If only because I am familiar with its embrace. . .

A THOUGHT #5

To have been so loved is far more painful a thing than to have been hated.

A THOUGHT #6

Hopelessness is being angry at nothing and no one and somehow the whole world all at once. . .

A THOUGHT #7

Depression is leaving most of yourself in bed every morning while the rest of you desperately struggles to keep your life from falling apart.

A THOUGHT #8

More reason for my life escapes me.

Than you, who seeks with love, to encase me.

Alone and unguided, I made by force to end my strife.

Then you enter, and, unwittingly, save my life. . .

A THOUGHT #9

Life after life, we spend filling the endless void
with angry, heated words.
So that now, at souls' end, we are left with nothing
but monochrome memory, with which to compose our swan song.
And so,
to this,
we must dance,
slowly,
Our final number. . .

A THOUGHT #10

Defeat is knowing that no one else could ever match the viciousness and vitriol with which we address ourselves in our own minds.

A THOUGHT #11

Apathy, so much stronger than hate.

Evict fools from your heart, Erase them from your mind.

You are strength.

And revenge?

Revenge is for the weak.

A THOUGHT #12

Don't feel bad when they don't understand you.
You are an open book, written in a foreign language.
And maybe no one ever taught them how to read anyway. . .
It's sad really, how small the world must be for them.

A THOUGHT #13

I find in my heart, I cannot forgive, those who deny me the right
to live.

Though, this stubborn nature is double-bladed.

It is only the outside of me that is so jaded.

A THOUGHT #14

Who are they,
these gods who rule us?
Unknown and unknowing.
Useless constructs of the desperate mind.
Humanities' last futile defense against an ever-encroaching abyss
we fail to recognize as our own imaginings. . .

A THOUGHT #15

She called to me, the mother earth,
"Come home my child, you've proved your worth."

A THOUGHT #16

She ran, I think, to heaven's gate.
Unwilling, or unable, to rid her heart of hate.

A THOUGHT #17

The dreams you stand on are stronger than they look. . .

A THOUGHT #18

The weight on your shoulders is heavy enough without the armor you think you need. . .

A THOUGHT #19

I sow the seeds of empire in the ashes of the bridges I've burned.

A THOUGHT #20

We are never who we were before.
I think every day we are something new. . .
and something more.

A THOUGHT #21

Sometimes my body feels so heavy I think my heart might stop. . .

A THOUGHT #22

They want from you what you cannot give,
They want your soul and your will to live. . .